# F-16 Fighting Falcon

### 3rd Edition

*To the Fighting Falcon pilots who flew in Operation Desert Storm—and to the men and women who kept them flying.*

# F-16 Fighting Falcon

### 3rd Edition

## Bill Siuru and Bill Holder

TAB AERO

Blue Ridge Summit, PA

Aero series

42

THIRD EDITION
SECOND PRINTING

© 1991 by **TAB/AERO Books,** an imprint of TAB Books.
TAB Books is a division of McGraw-Hill, Inc.

**Library of Congress Cataloging-in-Publication Data**

Siuru, William D.
    F-16 Fighting Falcon / by Bill Siuru and Bill Holder.—3rd ed.
      p.  cm.—(Aero series : v. 42)
    Rev. ed. of: General Dynamics F-16 Fighting Falcon / William D.
Siuru, Jr. and William G. Holder. 2nd ed. 1983.
    ISBN 0-8306-3425-8 (p)
    I. Holder, William G., 1937–  .  II. Siuru, William D.  General
Dynamics F-16 Fighting Falcon.  III. Title.
UG1242.F5S575  1991
358.4′382—dc20                         91-8589
                                          CIP

TAB Books offers software for sale. For information and a catalog, please contact TAB Software Department, Blue Ridge Summit, PA 17294-0850.

Acquisitions Editor: Jeff Worsinger
Book Editor: Steven H. Mesner
Production: Katherine G. Brown
Series Design: Jaclyn J. Boone
                AS1

# Contents

# Foreword

THE F-16 IS a winner—and it makes winners of the pilots who fly it and the maintenance personnel who keep it ready. The Fighting Falcon has been an exciting aircraft from its inception, and it promises to be a dazzling performer well into the 21st century.

As the F-16 Program Director, I have the distinct privilege of carrying on the F-16's legacy of superb performance, unprecedented mission capable rates, and continuous technology upates. Through our Multinational Staged Improvement Program (MSIP), we have continuously modernized F-16s with new avionics, advanced armaments, and enhanced reliability. The Block 40 airplanes being delivered today provide our Tactical Air Forces with a revolutionary night attack capability through the incorporation of LANTIRN (Low-Altitude Navigation and Targeting Infrared System for Night).

While we are delivering those aircraft, we are in Full Scale Development for the next version of the F-16, the Block 50, which will start deliveries in October 1991. We are in the planning stages for a Close Air Support (CAS) variant, designated F/A-16, to begin deliveries in mid-1996. Concurrently, we are working with our four European partners on an upgrade to F-16A/B's called Mid-Life Update and with Tactical Air Command on a CAS upgrade to Block 30 airplanes as well as incorporating a reconnaissance capability into RF-16s. In essence, these enhancements to the very capable F-16 airframe are keeping this versatile multi-role fighter forever young.

The F-16 is a success story with the USAF, the U.S. Navy, and 15 foreign countries. I know you will enjoy reading about it.

BGen. Ralph H. Graham
Program Director,
F-16 System Program Office

# Acknowledgments

THE AUTHORS wish to thank the following organizations and individuals for their con-tributions and help in preparing this book.

Ford Aerospace & Communications Corporation.

General Dynamics Corporation in Fort Worth, Texas; St. Louis, Missouri; and Dayton, Ohio.

General Electric Company.

Hughes Aircraft Company.

McDonnell Douglas Corporation.

Naval Weapons Center.

Northrop Corporation.

Pratt & Whitney Aircraft.

Raytheon Company.

SAAB-Scania Aktiebolag.

SABCA.

United States Air Force, especially Mike Wallace (not *that* Mike Wallace) of the Public Affairs Office at the Aeronautical Systems Division, Wright-Patterson AFB, Ohio; and the Arnold Engineering Development Center, Tennessee.

United States Navy.

Andrea and Brian Siuru for proofreading the manuscript.

# Introduction

ALMOST TWO decades have passed since the U.S. Air Force laid the groundwork for what would eventually become the F-16 Fighting Falcon. Since then, this versatile fighter has proven itself to be one of the world's all-time great aircraft. But its story is far from over. The F-16 will be serving well into the 21st century, taking on even more challenging roles and missions. It will also see new markings as other countries choose the F-16 for their own Air Forces.

This third edition is but another chapter in the F-16 story, with more chapters undoubtedly still to come. The first two editions should be consulted by those interested in more detail on the F-16's earlier history.

# 1

# Birth of the Fighting Falcon

FROM A FIGHTER pilot's point of view, his aircraft has to be judged on how well it stands up against the fighters of his enemy. The machine must be an extension of the pilot, responding instantaneously to his every demand. It must be agile and maneuverable. Most of all, it must be dependable!

The top fighters of World War I had these qualities. World War I fighters such as the Sopwith Camel and the SPAD, and later the Mustang and Spitfire of World War II are legends in aviation history. These aircraft all pushed the state of the art of aviation technology for their time periods and showed their stuff with outstanding kill ratios over the enemy.

This is the story of a current fighter with the same attributes. It's the F-16 Fighting Falcon, the "fighter pilot's fighter." It is a fighter aircraft that was designed in the 1970s but that will be around well into the 21st century.

## The Lightweight Fighter

When it comes right down to it, the easiest way to make a fighter lethal and agile is to make it *light*: Make it small, and give it a gutsy power plant that operates economically so as to reduce the fuel load. Strip out all but the essential electronic equipment.

It sounds easy, but it's not always easy to do.

In the years after World War II, American fighters increased in size and weight at an amazing rate. More equipment was added as the aircraft were given more jobs to do—multi-mission capability is what the military calls it. This trend continued until some of the modern fighter aircraft weighed more than the bombers of World War II.

*Lightweight fighters of two different eras. The North American P-51 Mustang was the fighter of World War II, while the F-16 Fighting Falcon is the fighter of the 1980s and 1990s—and maybe beyond!*

By the early 1970s, the need was seen to try to reverse this trend. The United States Air Force made a bold step in that direction when the so-called Lightweight Fighter Program was born in 1972. The USAF had an added incentive for the program: It is a well-known fact that aircraft *costs* can usually be related directly to the weight of the plane, so all things being equal, a *lighter* aircraft should be a *less expensive* machine. With the cost of fighters such as the F-15 Eagle already at about $15 million a copy in 1972, the Air Force knew that the next fighter down the line was going to have to cost significantly less.

The F-16 was not, of course, the first "lightweight fighter" in history. There were several lightweight designs from Europe in the 1920s and '30s. These included the wooden Caudron C.714 and Bloch M.B. 700 from the French. The British developed the M.20 with an armament of 12 guns.

During World War II, the United States had to play catch-up with the enemy in both theaters of the war. Impressed with the enemy's successes with lightweight, quick fighters such as the Japanese Zero and German BF-109, and aware of forecasted shortages of air-

*Here is another interesting inflight comparison between one of World War II's best Navy fighters, the F4U Corsair, and the F-16.*

craft materials, the Army Air Corps started to get serious about building a light fighter of its own. The requirements for the new fighter that were given to Bell Aircraft in 1941 sounded a lot like the initial specifications of the F-16 that would evolve some 30 years later. The contract called for a "lightweight, inexpensive, highly maneuverable fighter."

The aircraft that resulted from those guidelines was a strange-looking machine carrying the designation of XP-77. The little fighter had a personality all its own with a squatty fuselage that looked nose-heavy, a bubble canopy, and tricycle landing gear.

Problems during the light fighter's development program delayed its first flight until 1944. By that time, advances in aeronautical technology had passed by the XP-77. Already improved versions of the P-47 Thunderbolt and P-51 Mustang were in the thick of the air war and there was no place for the little lightweight fighter as the war finally wound down.

During the 1950s and '60s, thoughts of a lightweight fighter were lost as the "Century Series" fighters from the F-100 through F-106 grew heavier and heavier. It took some lessons from the light, highly-maneuverable Soviet MiGs of the Korean and Vietnam Wars to prove again that the lightweight fighter was still a viable concept. But it would not be until the 1970s that the F-16 would be born.

Like many other things, the term "lightweight" is only a relative one. Back in the 1940s, when the P-51 and P-47 weighed out at about five and ten tons respectively, the Zero and BF-109 each weighed considerably less than three tons. In comparison, the eight-to-ten ton MiGs were considerably lighter than the American opposition. Today, the 23,600-pound F-16 is considerably smaller than the other recent additions to the United States fighter force.

*The first YF-16 prototype carried a very patriotic red, white, and blue paint scheme. The plane was a winner in many ways including being the victor in the flyoff competition against the Northrop YF-17.*

*The YF-17, competitor to the YF-16, was a twin-engined aircraft with a considerably different planform. Without a doubt, it too was an excellent aircraft and quickly got the attention of the Navy, which favors twin-engine on its carrier-based fighters.*

*The YF-17 would eventually evolve into the Navy's F-18 fighter, which would be deployed on aircraft carriers as a replacement for the A-7 Corsair II. Like the F-16, the F-18 would also be purchased by a number of foreign countries.*

## Lightweight Contenders

The prototype procurement approach was a new scheme that the Department of Defense was applying to the acquisition of new weapon systems when the Lightweight Fighter Program was in full swing. Rather than having to base the decision to go into production on paper studies and designs, as had been done with most of the Air Force's more recent aircraft, the idea was to build one or more prototypes, test them extensively under operational conditions, and then decide whether or not to go into full-scale production. The idea of prototyping was not new; this was the way just about every aircraft was acquired by the Army Air Corps during the period between the World Wars.

When the USAF's Aeronautical Systems Division at Wright-Patterson Air Force Base, Ohio, asked for proposals to build lightweight prototype fighters, five aerospace companies responded with proposals. These were General Dynamics, Boeing, Lockheed, LTV Aerospace, and Northrop. The experts mulled over the proposals in great depth, fully realizing that the winner could well be awarded one of the biggest aircraft contracts ever.

Finally, it was announced that General Dynamics and Northrop were the winners of the competition. Each company would build two prototypes, then the two designs would compete in a flyoff to determine which the Air Force would put into production. General Dynamics would build their proposed single-engine YF-16, while Northrop would go

*The "Y" was shed from the prototype's tail after the F-16 became the winner of the fighter shootout. During its early days, this was one of the most publicized fighters ever built.*

*The second YF-16 prototype carried the tail number 568. Initially, the plane was painted with an unique camouflage scheme that was never adopted for operational aircraft.*

*The two YF-16 prototypes show off their two different paint schemes.*

with the dual-engine YF-17. The lightweight fighter was becoming a reality.

On December 13, 1973, the red, white, and blue YF-16 prototype was rolled out of the hangar at the General Dynamics plant in Fort Worth, Texas. This first F-16 was ready for flight less than two years after the prototype go-ahead decision. In the modern era of super-complex aircraft, this was an accomplishment of amazing proportions.

Several weeks after that initial rollout, the prototype F-16 was dismantled enough to fit through the nose door of a giant C-5 Galaxy transport. The YF-16 was then flown to Edwards Air Force Base, California, to begin the flight test portion of the flyoff with the competing YF-17.

## First Flights

It would not be a great beginning, though, for the YF-16. During the testing of January 20, 1974, the aircraft took to the air for the first time with General Dynamics engineering test pilot Phil Oestricher at the controls—but the flight was not a part of the planned mission of that day. It happened during what was planned as a high-speed taxi test when the YF-16 sustained minor damage to its right horizontal stabilizer. Oestricher elected to take off rather than attempt to stop the aircraft. He flew the YF-16 for six minutes without any problems and ended the flight with a routine and normal landing.

The first *planned* flight occurred several days later (on February 4), again with Oestricher at the stick. This time he flew the new fighter for 90 minutes. After a routine take-off, he climbed to 15,000 feet and then cycled the landing gear. With the gear up, he took the YF-16 up to 30,000 feet at a speed of 300 knots. At this altitude, he performed pitch, roll, and yaw maneuvers and made a number of 3G turns. It was quite evident that the new bird was some machine!

The second YF-16 was delivered to Edwards on February 27, again by a C-5. This second prototype was painted in a camouflage pattern of sky blue and cloud white. This color pattern was intended to allow the aircraft to blend in with the sky, making it difficult for an enemy fighter or ground-based missiles to spot. The camouflage scheme would later be dropped as ineffective and was replaced with a dull gray paint scheme.

Both Air Force and General Dynamics pilots participated in the flight test program. The USAF pilots were from the Air Force Systems Command, the organization responsi-

7

*The two YF-16 prototypes in flight.*

*The first F-16 prototype does its stuff against the aircraft it will eventually replace, the F-4. The F-16 can outmaneuver the venerable Phantom.*

ble for developing new aircraft, and from the Tactical Air Command, which would be the ultimate user of the aircraft. There was an identical situation for the YF-17 competitor, with both Northrop and USAF test pilots involved.

*In 1978, testing at General Dynamic's Fort Worth facility simulated two full lifetimes without the aircraft ever leaving the ground. The purpose of the testing was to locate and correct any areas of the airframe that might be susceptible to fatigue before the first aircraft was delivered to the USAF. In the test rig, the F-16 was subjected to 16,000 hours of simulated flight using over 100 computed-controlled, hydraulically-driven pressure rams.*

The Air Force's flight test crews were broken into three teams. One team flew each contender about an equal share of flight time, while each of the other teams concentrated on one aircraft or the other. On the basis of the evaluations and reports of these test pilots, the test force made its recommendations from both technical and performance points of view as to which of the two craft should be built. It was a unanimous decision that the YF-16 was the best of the two fighters to satisfy the Air Force requirements.

The following February, the current Secretary of the Air Force, John Lucas, made the announcement that the F-16 was the winner in the so-called Air Combat competition and that production of the F-16 could commence immediately. He made the following comments about the program:

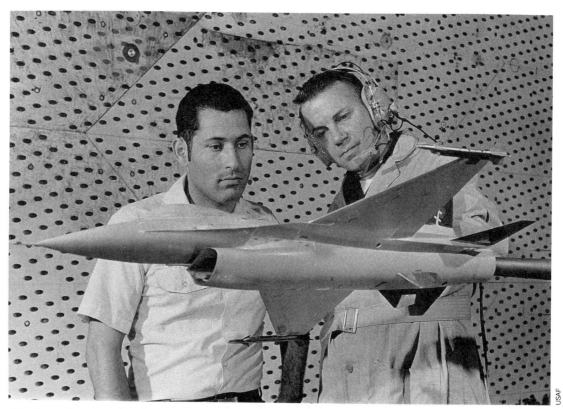

*Wind tunnel testing played a key role in proving the F-16's aerodynamic design. Here a scale model of the F-16 is tested in one of the wind tunnels at the USAF's Arnold Engineering Development Center (AEDC).*

*This is one of the first F-16s delivered to the USAF for Operational Testing and Evaluation (OT&E). Note the flags of a number of countries that would be buying and using the F-16.*

# YF-16 PROTOTYPE FLIGHT TEST PROGRAM

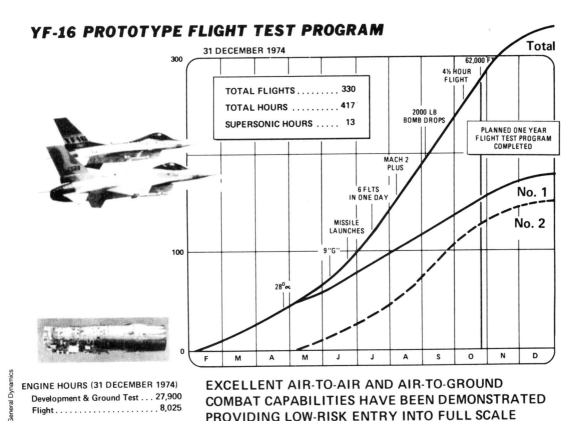

**31 DECEMBER 1974**

| TOTAL FLIGHTS | 330 |
| TOTAL HOURS | 417 |
| SUPERSONIC HOURS | 13 |

62,000 FT

4½ HOUR FLIGHT

**Total**

2000 LB BOMB DROPS

PLANNED ONE YEAR FLIGHT TEST PROGRAM COMPLETED

MACH 2 PLUS

6 FLTS IN ONE DAY

**No. 1**

MISSILE LAUNCHES

**No. 2**

9 "G"

28° α

General Dynamics

ENGINE HOURS (31 DECEMBER 1974)
Development & Ground Test ... 27,900
Flight ........................ 8,025

**EXCELLENT AIR-TO-AIR AND AIR-TO-GROUND COMBAT CAPABILITIES HAVE BEEN DEMONSTRATED PROVIDING LOW-RISK ENTRY INTO FULL SCALE DEVELOPMENT AND PRODUCTION.**

*The flight test program using the two YF-16 prototypes was one of the most successful test programs ever conducted.*

"The flight test program that was conducted was an evaluation of two very fine fighters. Both of the aircraft performed very well. Both of the contractors did an excellent job of supporting the prototype test program. Both of the engine companies (General Electric and Pratt & Whitney) did an excellent job of supporting the aircraft companies. On the other hand, there were significant differences in the performance of the two prototypes. The YF-16 had many advantages over the YF-17. It had advantages in performance, along with advantages in agility, acceleration, turn rate, and endurance. These factors applied principally in the transonic and supersonic regimes. There were other advantages in the areas of better tolerances of high Gs because of the tilt-back seat, along with better visibility and better acceleration."

All would not be lost with the YF-17, however, as it would eventually evolve into the Navy's F-18 Hornet, an aircraft that has met all the U.S. Navy's requirements and has been exported to several foreign countries.

But this was the hour for General Dynamics and the F-16. The F-16 design had been proved by the flight testing and now it was time for the fighter to prove that it could do the job in service with the USAF—including combat.

**11**

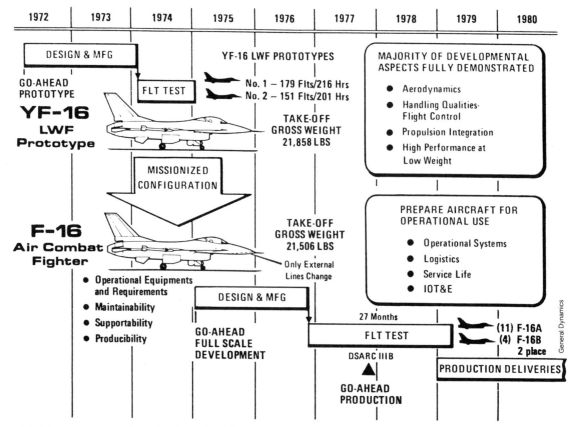

| 1972 | 1973 | 1974 | 1975 | 1976 | 1977 | 1978 | 1979 | 1980 |
|------|------|------|------|------|------|------|------|------|

**DESIGN & MFG**

GO-AHEAD
PROTOTYPE

**FLT TEST**

YF-16 LWF PROTOTYPES

No. 1 – 179 Flts/216 Hrs
No. 2 – 151 Flts/201 Hrs

**YF-16**
**LWF**
**Prototype**

TAKE-OFF
GROSS WEIGHT
21,858 LBS

**MAJORITY OF DEVELOPMENTAL
ASPECTS FULLY DEMONSTRATED**

- Aerodynamics
- Handling Qualities-
  Flight Control
- Propulsion Integration
- High Performance at
  Low Weight

**MISSIONIZED
CONFIGURATION**

**F-16**
**Air Combat**
**Fighter**

TAKE-OFF
GROSS WEIGHT
21,506 LBS

Only External
Lines Change

**PREPARE AIRCRAFT FOR
OPERATIONAL USE**

- Operational Systems
- Logistics
- Service Life
- IOT&E

- Operational Equipments
  and Requirements
- Maintainability
- Supportability
- Producibility

**DESIGN & MFG**

GO-AHEAD
FULL SCALE
DEVELOPMENT

27 Months

**FLT TEST**

DSARC IIIB

▲

**GO-AHEAD
PRODUCTION**

(11) F-16A
(4) F-16B
2 place

**PRODUCTION DELIVERIES**

General Dynamics

*F-16 development and production schedule.*

12

# 2

# Fighting Falcon Specifications

MANY MILITARY experts say the F-16 is the best fighter aircraft in the world. That's an amazing statement when one considers that the aircraft was designed in the 1970s and the statement still holds true in the 1990s. Versatility is the name of the game with the Fighting Falcon, as the aircraft has evolved into a machine capable of doing may jobs—and doing them all well.

Even in the early 1990s, the F-16 continues to get better and better as new models and variants appear. Hundreds have been bought by the U.S. Air Force and by an ever-increasing number of countries around the world as well. When production of the F-16 is finally completed, it could well be the most-produced fighter in the history of aviation—at least in the jet age. In an era of hugely expensive military aircraft, the F-16 remains an attractive option. In fact, future variants of the Fighting Falcon could replace new aircraft that are today still in the design phase!

## The F-16 Described

Even though many different versions of the F-16 have been produced or are planned, there are some generic statements that can be made about the aircraft. It's slightly over 49 feet in length—short by today's standards—and has a wingspan of almost 33 feet. From the ground to the tip of the vertical tail, the F-16 measures 16.4 feet.

The early versions of the F-16 had a gross takeoff weight of about 23,600 pounds, with a maximum takeoff weight of about 35,400 pounds. These weights, however, have changed as different weapons and electronics packages have been added to the sleek fighting machine.

The F-16 is powered by the Pratt & Whitney F100-PW-200. This is essentially the same engine used in the McDonnell Douglas F-15 Eagle, a selection which certainly saved a massive amount of money on development as well as maintenance and spare parts inventory due to commonality. The F100 is in the 25,000-pound thrust class and supplies 25 percent more thrust per pound than previous engines. Its 10-stage compressor is driven by a two-stage turbine, while the three-stage turbofan is driven by two additional stages of the turbine. The engine is 191 inches long, weighs slightly over 3,000 pounds, and is almost 35 inches in diameter at the engine inlet.

*The lifting-body fuselage of the F-16 is very apparent from this angle. Instead of the wings being attached to a cylindrical fuselage, the wing roots seem to be a part of the fuselage. It's become the aerodynamic shape of the fighter plane.*

## High-Tech, Low-Tech

Advanced technology is found in almost every portion of the F-16 power plant. The advanced components coupled with extensive use of high-technology materials make the engine lighter and able to produce more thrust—actually about eight pounds of thrust for every pound of engine weight. The F100 is almost completely smokeless, making detection by the enemy very difficult, if not impossible.

# F-16A & F-16B Are Identical Dimensionally

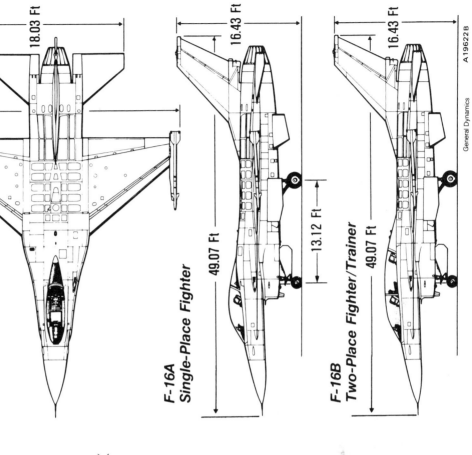

18.03 Ft

32.83

**F-16A**
*Single-Place Fighter*

16.43 Ft

49.07 Ft

13.12 Ft

**F-16B**
*Two-Place Fighter/Trainer*

16.43 Ft

49.07 Ft

A19622B

General Dynamics

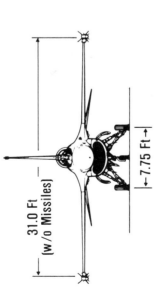

31.0 Ft
[w/o Missiles]

7.75 Ft

Wing Area . . . . . . . . . . . . . . .300 Sq Ft
Aspect Ratio . . . . . . . . . . . . . . .3.0
L.E. Sweep . . . . . . . . . . . . . . . .40º
Design Load Factor. . . . . . . . . . 9''g''
Design T.O.G.W. . . . . . . . . 22,500 lb
Max T.O.G.W . . . . . . . . . . 35,400 lb
Max Ext Load Capacity. . . . 15,200 lb

*Basic dimensions for the F-16.*

*The F100 jet engine has been produced in huge numbers by Pratt & Whitney over the years. In this photo, a number of P&W employees celebrated the production of the 2,000th of these powerful engines.*

The F-16 is constructed of lightweight materials, but not highly exotic ones. The aircraft's structure is 80 percent aluminum, a material that probably wouldn't have been used as extensively if the F-16 were being designed in the 1990s. Titanium and composites make up less than 10 percent of the structure, and these special materials were used only where they were absolutely needed to do the job.

Another cost-saving aspect of the design of the F-16 was the use of identical and interchangeable horizontal tail surfaces, ventral fins, and flap/ailerons. Additionally, 80 percent of the landing gear is interchangeable from port to starboard side.

When you really get right down to it, the F-16 looks more like a "lifting body" spacecraft than a manned interceptor. The Falcon's stubby wings, which join the fuselage far back on the fuselage, have a surface area of only 300 square feet and a 40-degree sweepback. The tail surfaces have basically the same shape, but with a slight droop. The F-16's external appearance is the result of the blended wing-body design adopted for the aircraft. This aerodynamic configuration provides lift from its shape at high angles of attack, gives less wetted surface area (thus less drag), provides more internal fuel storage capacity, and results in a more rigid structure.

# PRATT & WHITNEY AIRCRAFT

## F100-PW-100 AUGMENTED TURBOFAN ENGINE

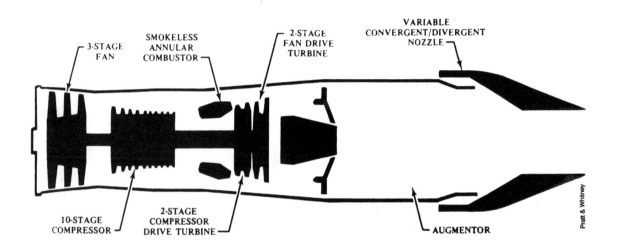

CHARACTERISTICS:

| | |
|---|---|
| MAXIMUM THRUST (FULL AUGMENTATION) | 25,000-POUND (111.2 kN) CLASS |
| INTERMEDIATE THRUST (NON—AUGMENTED) | 15,000-POUND (66.7 kN) CLASS |
| WEIGHT | 3,020 POUNDS (1371 kg) |
| LENGTH | 191 INCHES (4.85 m) |
| INLET DIAMETER | 36 INCHES (0.91 m) |
| MAXIMUM DIAMETER | 46.5 INCHES (1.18 m) |
| BYPASS RATIO | 0.6 |
| OVERALL PRESSURE RATIO | 24 to 1 |

HISTORY:

| | |
|---|---|
| DESIGN BEGAN | AUGUST 1968 |
| DEVELOPMENT CONTRACT AWARD | MARCH 1970 |
| PRELIMINARY FLIGHT RATING TEST (PFRT) COMPLETED | FEBRUARY 1972 |
| FIRST FLIGHT | JULY 1972 |
| QUALIFICATIONS TEST (QT) COMPLETED | OCTOBER 1973 |
| FLIGHT TIME (THROUGH JANUARY 1975) | 8,500 HOURS |
| TOTAL DEVELOPMENT TEST TIME (THROUGH JANUARY 1975) | 32,000 HOURS |
| OPERATIONAL INTRODUCTION (LUKE AIR FORCE BASE) | NOVEMBER 1974 |

*Specifications for the F100 engine.*

*Two F100 engines are readied for shipment for installation in F-16 fighters.*

*The F-16B was the logical follow-on to the initial F-16A. All the dimensions of the B version remained the same with the exception of the lengthened canopy.*

All these advantages were amazingly accomplished with reduced structure weight, a significant engineering accomplishment. The additional lift from the body configuration is needed at high angles of attack, because the lift contribution from the wings at this attitude begins to fall off. The wings incorporate leading and trailing edge flaps (called flaperons) that automatically change their contour to suit the angle of attack or speed of the airplane. This gives a maximum lift-to-drag ratio and minimum buffeting during all flight regimes.

*The F-16 can carry an impressive assortment of weapons. However, it is obvious that they can't all be carried at the same time.*

## From the Driver's Seat

The F-16 pilot uses a fly-by-wire control system to fly the aircraft. Here the normal mechanical linkages, cables, and bellcranks were replaced by wires that carry the electrical commands from the pilot's controls to individual actuators that move the control surfaces. The new-at-the-time system offers better handling qualities, more precise and responsive control (essential in combat), increased reliability and survivability, and a simplified aircraft structure with more room for all-important fuel. There is no mechanical backup for the wire-controlled systems, but there are four separate channels for the electrical signals to make their way from the pilot's hands to the necessary actuators.

In order to perform maneuvers with great precision, even under the stress of high Gs, the pilot flies the craft using a sidestick controller. This device replaces the conventional

*This F-16A is carrying a full load of weapons including Sidewinder missiles on its wingtips.*

*This F-16A, carrying a load of inert weapons, is about to initiate a pass on one of the extensive gunnery and bombing ranges in the western desert areas of the United States.*

20

# Production and cost considerations

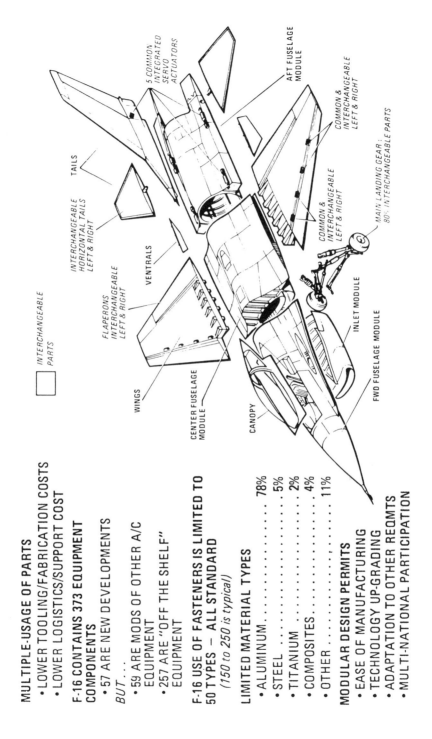

INTERCHANGEABLE PARTS

**MULTIPLE-USAGE OF PARTS**
- LOWER TOOLING/FABRICATION COSTS
- LOWER LOGISTICS/SUPPORT COST

**F-16 CONTAINS 373 EQUIPMENT COMPONENTS**

*BUT ....*
- 57 ARE NEW DEVELOPMENTS
- 59 ARE MODS OF OTHER A/C EQUIPMENT
- 257 ARE "OFF THE SHELF" EQUIPMENT

**F-16 USE OF FASTENERS IS LIMITED TO 50 TYPES — ALL STANDARD**
*(150 to 250 is typical)*

**LIMITED MATERIAL TYPES**
- ALUMINUM . . . . . . . . . . . . . . 78%
- STEEL . . . . . . . . . . . . . . . . . . 5%
- TITANIUM . . . . . . . . . . . . . . . 2%
- COMPOSITES . . . . . . . . . . . . . 4%
- OTHER . . . . . . . . . . . . . . . . . 11%

**MODULAR DESIGN PERMITS**
- EASE OF MANUFACTURING
- TECHNOLOGY UP-GRADING
- ADAPTATION TO OTHER REQMTS
- MULTI-NATIONAL PARTICIPATION

Labels in figure: INTERCHANGEABLE HORIZONTAL TAILS LEFT & RIGHT; TAILS; 5 COMMON INTEGRATED SERVO ACTUATORS; AFT FUSELAGE MODULE; COMMON & INTERCHANGEABLE LEFT & RIGHT; COMMON & INTERCHANGEABLE LEFT & RIGHT; MAIN LANDING GEAR: 80% INTERCHANGEABLE PARTS; FLAPERONS INTERCHANGEABLE LEFT & RIGHT; VENTRALS; WINGS; CENTER FUSELAGE MODULE; CANOPY; INLET MODULE; FWD FUSELAGE MODULE

General Dynamics

*F-16 production and cost considerations. Note the low usage of exotic materials and composites.*

**21**

center-mounted stick. The pilot's arm is on the support armrest; by using very slight hand pressure, he sends the electrical signals through the fly-by-wire system to the control surfaces.

Due to the extreme maneuverability of the F-16, special consideration was given to the design of the cockpit. To that end, the seat angle is a rather laid-back—literally!—30 degrees. By sitting in a more reclined position, the pilot's tolerance to high Gs is greatly increased.

The F-16 is also equipped with a bubble canopy that allows the pilot almost unlimited visibility—360 degrees available in the horizontal direction, 260 degrees side-to-side, 195 degrees fore-and-aft, 40 degrees down over the side and 15 degrees over the nose. The canopy is fabricated of polycarbonate, a virtually indestructible plastic material.

A device that certainly has the positive vote of the F-16 pilot is the triple-redundant emergency egress system. It ensures his safe departure from the plane. If all systems fail, the pilot can unlatch the canopy and push it into the airstream.

The F-16 can carry a wide variation of weapon loads. There are six different configurations including Dogfight, Long-Range Interception, Strike, Ground Attack, Wild Wea-

General Dynamics

*Aerial view of the General Dynamics Fort Worth Division's facility. This is one of the world's largest aircraft manufacturing plants. Since 1942, over 7000 military airplanes have been produced on its mile-long assembly line.*

*Two products built at the Fort Worth facility, the B-24 Liberator bomber of World War II fame and the F-16.*

*Looking down the F-16 production line at the General Dynamics Fort Worth plant. This production line should be active building F-16s for the USAF and other countries well past the mid-1990s.*

sel, and Precision Attack. In the Dogfight role, the F-16 carries two AIM-9L Sidewinders and the 20mm M61 Vulcan cannon. On the Long-Range mission, two AIM-7 Sparrow missiles are added to the armament.

For the strike mission, the weapons are two Mk83 1,000-pound bombs on the mid-wing pylons. Ground attack normally employs two Mk82 Snakeye 500-pound retarded bombs and two Sidewinders. The Wild Weasel mission carries two AGM-78 anti-radar missiles and two Sidewinders, while the Precision Attack mounts two Paveway laser guided bombs and two Sidewinders.

The first operational versions of the Fighting Falcon were the single-seat F-16A and the dual-seat F-16B. These achieved operational status with the Tactical Air Command in 1979 at Hill Air Force Base, Utah. Production of these first versions lasted until 1985.

# 3

# Improving the Breed

L IKE MANY other modern fighters, the F-16 has been modified and improved through the years. Still other modifications have been proposed, developed, and even tested, but often have not gone into production usually because of budgetary constraints. These programs are aimed at ensuring that the F-16 remains a versatile, highly capable, front-line fighter throughout its long service life, which will extend well into the next century.

## OCU

Many improvements to the F-16 have come as part of the Operational Capabilities Upgrade (OCU) program, which made improvements in the fire control, stores management, and computation capabilities. The main reasoning behind these upgrades was to make the F-16 compatible with the next generation of weapon systems.

## MSIP

Along the same lines, another set of improvements came in 1980 with the Multinational Staged Improvement Program (MSIP), which enabled the F-16 to accept new weapon systems under development, thus decreasing the cost that would be required to modify the aircraft when the time for incorporation actually takes place.

## ADF

In the late 1980s, another modification took place for the A and B model Falcons with the ADF modification. The ADF-modified F-16s are used for the air defense mission replacing, the F-106 and F-4 fighters that have been in service for many years. Besides the

F-16 cockpit layout for the MSIP Stage II aircraft. The wide angle HUD gives four times the instantaneous viewing area of early HUD design. Critical flight, weapon, and sensor information is displayed on the two multifunctional displays.

S/N 83-118 was the first F-16C model produced. The honor is duly noted by the notation "F-16C No. 1" displayed on the aircraft's fuselage.

20mm Vulcan gun, the ADF F-16 also carries up to six missiles of several types. The program is expected to be completed by 1991. In all, as many as 270 A and B models could be modified before the end of the program.

## F-16C/D

The two newest versions of the Fighting Falcon are the F-16C and F-16D models, the D being the two-seat variant. Deliveries of these versions began in 1984. While the F-16C and D resemble the A/B versions in appearance and share their high performance, there are many mostly internal improvements for greatly improved capability in combat. The improvements are especially oriented for beyond visual range (BVR) air-to-air intercept and night/under-the-weather navigation and attack missions. Many of the changes occurred in the aircraft's avionics and cockpit equipment.

From a performance standpoint, the engine inlet was redesigned for the F-16C/D. This results in improved high angle-of-attack stability and stall recovery characteristics. The new inlet, which is called the Modular Common Inlet Duct (MCID), is 12 inches wider than the original design.

One noticeable external change on the F-16C/D is the expanded tail root fairing designed to house two units of the ALQ-165 Airborne Self-Protection Jammer (ASPJ) internal electronic countermeasures set.

Structural changes were made to accommodate heavier gross weights. The F-16's unique 9-G capability at full internal fuel and basic air-to-air load was retained. Also, the maximum takeoff gross weight was increased from 35,400 to 37,500 pounds to accommodate increased external stores for fuel, ordnance, and sensors.

In the cockpit, there are two identical multifunction displays (MFDs) These video displays have arrays of software-controlled buttons around their periphery to display sensor video (radar, E-O, FLIR), symbology, and alphanumeric data. They also serve as control devices for sophisticated avionics equipment (radar, sensor pods, stores management, etc.). Control and display are integrated into a single unit for maximum ease of use. These MFDs replace a multitude of switches and knobs and provide almost unlimited growth capability for interfacing with future weapons, sensors, and avionic systems. The up-front controls allow the pilot quick and easy access to all communication, navigation, and identification functions without diverting attention from keeping track of "what's ahead."

A data transfer unit employs a solid-state cartridge for automatic loading of mission data (stores, navigation/target coordinates, radio frequencies, etc.). This eliminates the tedious and time-consuming task of manual entry, which can take up to 15 minutes. It also greatly reduces the chance of entry errors. This device also records in-flight mission data and any system faults for post-flight evaluation by operations and maintenance personnel.

The high-technology cockpit displays includes a FLIR (Forward Looking Infrared) display with raster video for superimposing FLIR imagery for night operation, and a wider angle head up display (HUD). One of the major goals in cockpit design was to reduce pilot workload, especially in the heat of battle.

Airframe changes include increased-capacity electrical power and cooling systems and wiring for "smart" weapons such as the AGM-65D Imaging Infrared Maverick, AIM-120A Advanced Medium Range Air-to-Air Missile (AMRAAM), anti-ship missiles, and anti-radiation missiles.

*The F-16D is the tandem-seat variant of the F-16C.*

## Block 30

In mid-1986, production F-16C/Ds (Block 30) were equipped with a configured engine bay to accommodate either of the Alternate Fighter Engines, the F100-PW-220 and F110-GE-100. These are considered the world's best fighter engines and incorporate many advanced technology features that provide significant benefits in operability, reliability, safety, durability, maintainability, and life cycle costs. Incidentally, while the USAF will be operating both engine types in its F-16C/Ds, foreign air forces have all selected one of the engines or the other for obvious maintenance reasons in their smaller fleets.

Another significant change made at Block 30 was seal-bonded fuselage fuel tanks to reduce the potential of fuel leaks. Other changes in this series include memory expansion of several core computers, software upgrades, a voice message unit, increased chaff/flare capacity, improved leading edge flap actuators, and a crash-survivable flight data recorder. The latter facilitates mishap investigation, service life monitoring, troubleshooting, and trend analysis, and has the potential to provide detailed playback for mission training and evaluation.

## Block 40

The USAF received its first Block 40 F-16C/D in December 1988. This version incorporates a new family of higher speed/capacity core avionics, a wider HUD employing diffractive optics, cockpit enhancements, a greatly enhanced gunsight, and the ability to interface with the space-based Global Positioning System (GPS).

There is also a digital flight control system with automatic terrain following, full integration of LANTIRN (Low Altitude Navigation and Targeting Infrared for Night) pods, and heavyweight landing gear (42,300 pounds maximum takeoff gross weight). The first 350 aircraft in this block series are to be assigned LANTIRN pods for night/under-the-weather precision navigation and attack. The targeting pod is mounted on one side of the engine inlet, while the navigation pod is carried on the other side.

## Block 50

In late 1991, another major production change is planned with the introduction of the Block 50 F-16C/Ds. Major changes will be made to the electronic warfare suite including advanced threat warning, advanced chaff/flare system, and full integration of HARM/ Shrike anti-radiation missiles. This version will also accommodate either of the Air Force's Increased Performance Engines (29,000-pound thrust class). Potential enhancements to cockpit utility, reliability, and maintainability are being evaluated for incorporation at this block change.

These second-generation F-16s include APG-68 fire control radar with a software-programmable signal processor and dual mode transmitter. In comparison to the A/B's APG-66, the APG-68 has greater range and resolution plus new modes of operation, such as track-while-scan for simultaneous 10-target tracking and moving target track for cueing of ground targets.

The avionics package also includes higher speed and larger memory computers for the fire control and stores management systems, plus new avionic architecture and software language. A radar altimeter provides improved flight safety at low altitudes and higher fire control system accuracy.

## F-16E?

There's even an F-16E down the road, which will continue to be improved over its earlier brothers. At the time of this writing in early 1991, it was uncertain whether this version would ever go into production. One thing *is* certain, however: It's certainly a far cry from the lightweight Fighting Falcon that first flew almost two decades earlier. Like most weapon systems, the F-16 has increased greatly in its technology content—and, unfortunately its cost as well—through the years.

# 4

# A World Fighter

EVERY DAY, more than 1500 Fighting Falcons take off from airfields on five continents. Currently F-16s are in service wearing the flags of some 16 countries around the world. While most of the several thousand F-16s have come from the mile-long assembly line at the General Dynamics Fort Worth Division, others have been produced at such diverse locations as Belgium and Turkey. The F-16s use parts coming from more than a dozen countries. The F-16 is more than a "fighter pilot's fighter," it is also a "world fighter." Eventually, more than 4,000 F-16s of all kinds and with all kinds of markings will be produced.

## The European Consortium

While the U.S. Air Force had to decide between the single-engine F-16 and the twin-engined Northrop F-17 for its new lightweight fighter in the mid-1970s, across the Atlantic the four-nation European Consortium had a larger selection of aircraft to choose from as a replacement for their aging Lockheed F-104s. The Consortium, comprising Belgium, the Netherlands, Denmark, and Norway, evaluated the Saab Viggen, the Dassault Mirage F.1, the YF-16, and the YF-17. In 1977, they decided on the F-16.

While the European contenders and the YF-17 were all fine aircraft, the F-16 had a lot going for it. The aircraft incorporated the latest in technology at the time it was designed, while the Saab and Mirage were relatively old designs. The Mirage F.1E was first flown in 1966 while the Viggen made its maiden flight in 1967. Although both of these candidates incorporated updated engines and avionics, the basic designs remained essentially unchanged. For example, the European aircraft lacked such features as fly-by-

*Here workers at the SABCA facility in Belgium attach the F-16's aluminum skin to the wing box.*

*Four F-16s being assembled at the SABCA facility in Belgium.*

*Belgium was the first foreign nation to fly the F-16.*

wire, side-stick controller, carbon composite components, and an advanced engine, all of which were found on the F-16.

Comparing the F-16 and the two European aircraft, the former offered better performance in just about every category with the possible exception of top speed. The Mirage could travel at speeds of up to Mach 2.5 versus the Mach 2 limit for the Viggen, F-16, and F-17. The F-16, though, could carry more payload, had a greater radius of action, and, mainly due to its higher G tolerance, was more maneuverable. In addition, the F-16 had the lowest fuel cost per flying hour and lower maintenance costs, giving it a substantial lead over the competition from a fiscal standpoint.

While the Europeans might have preferred a European-designed fighter, they could not overlook the fact that the U.S. was going to buy the aircraft in vast quantities. This meant a substantially lower per-plane cost since research and development and special tooling costs could be amortized over a larger number of aircraft.

Another factor to be considered was the fact that the Consortium's aircraft used in NATO would be flying alongside the USAF's F-16s. Thus there would be a standard fighter used throughout NATO. This was a goal the Europeans had been striving for in order to reduce logistics expense and complexity.

*Heavily loaded F-16 in use in the Netherlands.*

## European Production

But the clincher for the deal was the plan whereby F-16s purchased by the Consortium would be partially built and tested in the Consortium's own countries. Part of the deal between the American contractors involved in the F-16 program and the Europeans was a plan to minimize the actual flow of currency from Europe to the U.S. to pay for the aircraft by using "off-setting." Besides fabricating and assembling part of the European F-16s in Europe, a major portion of the cost for other aircraft and componentry would be "offset" by producing parts and assemblies for USAF aircraft as well as those purchased by other foreign countries.

Production of the F-16 was the first truly international aircraft program, with assembly taking place in three countries and component manufacturing in five. Through the years there has been some shifting of the production, but it still is a multinational program that has expanded to include even more countries.

While the first production F-16 was delivered to the U.S. Air Force in August 1978,

*Danish F-16.*

the F-16 production line at SONACA/SABCA in Belgium opened in early 1978 with a second line opening a few months later at Fokker-VFW in the Netherlands. The first European-built F-16 was assembled in Belgium and this F-16B made its maiden flight in December 1978 with Belgian test pilot Serge Martin at the stick and General Dynamics chief test pilot Neil Anderson in the rear seat.

## Other Foreign Falcons

The first operational F-16s were delivered to the Belgian and Dutch air forces in 1979. The Danish, Norwegian, and Israeli air forces got theirs in 1980. By 1982, Egypt and Pakistan were flying F-16s. Venezuela (1983), Korea (1989), Turkey (1987), Singapore (1988), Greece (1988) and Thailand (1988) followed. The latest countries to order the F-16 are Indonesia and Bahrain. As this book is being written, Portugal has just signed up for Fighting Falcons.

Other countries including Spain, Canada, and Australia have looked at the F-16; the latter two countries went for the F-18 instead. During the late 1970s, plans were underway

*Norwegian F-16 making an ''intercept''on a Soviet Backfire bomber.*

*F-16 in operation with the Israeli Air Force. The effective paint scheme allows the aircraft to blend well with its desert surroundings.*

*Egyptian F-16A.*

*Pakistani F-16s.*

for Iran to buy 160 F-16s, but the drastic change in the Iranian government with the overthrow of the Shah squelched the deal.

When the world's F-16 fleet reached its two millionth flight hour in September 1988, the occasion was celebrated appropriately by simultaneously taking off F-16s flown by pilots from Belgium, Denmark, the Netherlands, and Norway, plus the USAF stationed in Europe.

The 200th F-16 built was delivered to Singapore in February 1988.

## Foreign Production

There are now two versions of the F-16 in production and operation not only in the U.S., but in foreign countries as well. The F-16C/D is in service with the air forces of Israel, Egypt, the Republic of Korea, Turkey, and Greece.

Foreign countries not only fly F-16s, they also build them—or at least supply componentry for their production. With the industries of 11 nations jointly producing structures and equipment, the F-16 Multinational Coproduction Program is by far the largest program of its type in history. Nations involved besides the United States include Belgium, Denmark, The Netherlands, Norway, Korea, Turkey, Israel, Singapore, Indonesia, and Greece. While not part of the program, parts for the F-16 also come from suppliers in Canada, England, France, Germany, and Sweden. Besides the Fort Worth assembly line, there are F-16 assembly lines in Gosselies, Belgium, near Amsterdam, The Netherlands, and Ankara, Turkey.

*F-16 of the Venezuelan Air Force demonstrating some high-performance maneuvers.*

Incidentally, there is some "customizing" of the F-16s to meet each country's needs. For instance, the Norwegian and Venezuelan F-16s have been fitted with drag chutes for use on shorter runways. Israeli F-16A/Bs house a Loral Rapport ECM in an extension of the fin root fairing. Belgian F-16s are being retrofitted with the ESD Carapace ECM and those for Pakistan are fitted with Thompson-CSF Atlis laser designation pods. Norwegian F-16s carry the Penguin Mk.3 anti-shipping missile and Dutch aircraft use the Orpheus reconnaissance pods.

*Four Korean F-16s in flight over the Olympic Village in Seoul.*

One interesting foreign F-16 derivative is the joint U.S.-Japanese FS-X. In the fall of 1987 the Japanese Defense Agency announced its intentions to develop a new fighter to replace the Mitsubishi M-1. Initial plans called for Mitsubishi to build 100 to 170 aircraft in Japan.

The FS-X would be based on the F-16 with a larger fuselage for greater fuel capacity. The nose radome will be extended to provide more room for the avionics. The FS-X would sprout forward canards and the leading edge flaps would be made of materials that could absorb rather than reflect radar energy. New avionics include a Mitsubishi Electronics active phased-array radar and proposed weapons include four Mitsubishi ASM-2 anti-shipping missiles. One of the biggest controversies surrounding the program is the potential transfer of advanced American technology to the Japanese.

*Turkish F-16.*

*F-16 of the Singapore Air Force.*

*Thai Air Force F-16.*

# 5

# F-16 Variations

FIRST, AN AIRCRAFT has a basic configuration and mission. Then changes are made as the engineers attempt to improve the aircraft or adapt it to new missions. In these days of tight military budgets, as often as not, such modifications result in a new prototype that never reaches production. In other cases, the aircraft is used as a test bed to try out new propulsion, aerodynamic, or electronic concepts. Sometimes the aircraft might even be modified to the extent that it is hardly recognizable to demonstrate a whole new generation of technology through flight testing.

All these types of changes have occurred to the F-16 through the years, and in fact are still happening. Not only is the Fighting Falcon a great fighter, it is also a great "experimental laboratory" for testing new ideas.

## F-16XL

From an appearance standpoint, the F-16XL was by far the most different of all the F-16 modifications. This model employed a radically new "cranked-arrow" wing shape. In addition, the fuselage was stretched 56 inches, increasing the internal fuel capacity by a whopping 82 percent. There was also a gain of an additional 40 cubic feet to accommodate future avionics and sensor growth.

Two standard F-16s were modified to XL configuration at the General Dynamics facility. The F-16's modular construction and electronic fly-by-wire control system greatly simplified the modification process.

The XL's new wing had an area of 646 cubic feet—more than double that of the standard F-16. Graphite polyimide composite skins were used in the construction to provide

*Three F-16s with three different power plants. On the left is the standard F-16 with the Pratt & Whitney F100 engine. In the middle, an F-16 equipped with a more powerful General Electric F101 engine. On the right is an F-16 with the less potent General Electric J79 engine.*

*The three F-16s in flight. Neither the F-16/101 or the F-16/79 would ever go beyond the prototype stage.*

the strength and stiffness necessary for maximum wing performance.

Test pilots were impressed with the XL's performance and found very little degradation in performance even when carrying a full load of weapons and ordnance. The aircraft's large wing also made landing significantly easier than the standard F-16.

The second of the two XL prototypes was different from the first in that it was a two-seat version and powered by the GE F101 Derivative Fighter Engine.

General Dynamics

*The F-16 "economy model." The F-16/79 prototype was built to determine how well a lower-thrust General Electric J79 engine would perform in the F-16. The version was intended for the export market for countries that did not want the full-up F-16. There was little interest in this aircraft, since customer countries wanted the "real" F-16.*

It is obvious when observing the XL configuration that this aircraft really should no longer be called an F-16. The XL has been made so much larger, with a practically new fuselage and a *completely* new wing, that it's a whole new airplane.

Despite the excellent results of its flight test program, though, the XL was not put into production. In fact, following the completion of their testing, both XLs were placed into storage—and most people figured that storage would be permanent.

But that would not be the case. In early 1989, one of the XLs was brought out of storage for a new NASA test program. In this program, the aircraft was equipped with an experimental wing glove filled with thousands of tiny laser-cut holes which are connected to an air pump in the fuselage. The purpose of the testing is to accomplish uninterrupted laminar airflow over the wings during supersonic flight. If successful, the result would be reduced drag and ultimately reduced fuel consumption.

## AFTI/F-16

The longest-running of all the F-16 test programs has been the AFTI/F-16 (Advanced

The most distinctive feature of the F-16XL was its highly-swept arrow-shaped wing, with more than twice the wing area of the standard F-16. Combined with a 56-inch longer fuselage, the F-16XL could carry over 80 percent more fuel internally than the standard F-16.

The F-16XL had substantially greater range on internal fuel with twice the payload, or more than double the radius with equal payload.

Fighter Technology Integration) program managed by the Flight Dynamics Laboratory of the Air Force Systems Command. The motivation behind the AFTI was to build a test bed aircraft that could demonstrate in flight new technologies that allow the fighter pilot to operate his machine more efficiently. The emphasis is on demonstrating advanced fighter technologies for improved air-to-air and air-to-surface weapons delivery, as well as enhancing aircraft and pilot survivability.

General Dynamics was awarded the contract to build the AFTI/F-16 in late 1978. By 1982, the AFTI/F-16 was flight-testing a new triplex digital flight control system. These highly successful flight tests were done between the summer of 1982 and 1983 with 118 sorties and 177 flight test hours flown.

Next, the AFTI/F-16 was used in the ambitious Automated Maneuvering Attack System (AMAS) program, whose overall objective was to demonstrate new combat capabilities made possible by a high degree of automation and integration. After modification of the AFTI/F-16 aircraft by General Dynamics at Fort Worth, the aircraft was returned to NASA's Dryden Flight Research Facility at Edwards AFB for the AMAS flight test program, which ran from 1984 through 1987. The program—jointly sponsored by the Air Force, Army, Navy, and NASA—completed 237 sorties and accumulated nearly 400 hours of flight testing. Let us look at some of the technologies and advanced equipment flight tested in the AMAS program.

*Before building the AFTI/F-16, the design was extensively tested in the wind tunnel. Here engineers at the Arnold Engineering Development Center (AEDC) inspect the installation of the two forward vertical canards.*

In the air-to-surface weapon delivery mode, AMAS demonstrated an automated, high-G, curvilinear flight profile flown essentially "on the deck" that could be used to put munitions accurately on target. This scenario required the integration of such onboard equipment as the Low Altitude Radar Autopilot, the FLIR/laser sensor/tracker, Ground Collision Avoidance (GCA) system, HUD, and helmet-mounted sights. After the pilot designates the target using the FLIR display or with his helmet-mounted sight, the automated system takes over to steer the aircraft on the attack profile that ensures accurate weapons delivery. This is followed by an automated egress, at which point control of the aircraft is handed back over to the pilot.

An important safety-related technology demonstrated during AMAS was an automatic recovery technique using the autopilot, which could take over and fly the aircraft should the pilot black out because of G-induced loss of consciousness (or GLOC) experienced during high-G maneuvers. A GLOC problem is sensed if the aircraft descends through an altitude threshold preselected by the pilot. In other words, the aircraft is on a collision course with the ground.

In order to reduce pilot workload during critical maneuvers and combat, the military is interested in voice commands to replace hands-on operation of controls. Thus the AFTI/ F-16 was equipped with Voice Interactive Avionics to determine which cockpit functions are appropriate for voice command. Another important technology demonstrated in the AMAS was the Digital Terrain Management and Display System, which has the capability to digitally generate full-color maps at different scales.

Let us check out the F-16/AFTI's cockpit: Two display screens dominate the layout, each comprising a four-square-inch black-and-white cathode ray tube surrounded by 20 electronic pushbuttons. Two display generators draw the lines and write the symbols on the displays. These devices were designed to allow the pilot to interact with the aircraft's avionics and flight control system. Also displayed for the pilot are data from the radar and infrared sensor systems.

In addition to an advanced head-up display (HUD), there are four mission buttons for the four modes of operation (air-to-air guns, air-to-surface bombs, strafing, or missiles). By simply pushing one of these buttons, the pilot has the capability to engage all the aircraft systems that he needs for that particular mission. Automatic combat? The AFTI/F-16 comes pretty close!

After the AMAS program, the AFTI/F-16 was modified for its new role in demonstrating new close air support (CAS) technologies that will allow the Air Force to more effectively support troops on the ground. One of the first tasks was to investigate techniques for eliminating the need for voice communications between the close air support fighter and forward air controllers on the ground or target spotters in scout helicopters or other fighters.

In the program, digital information on the target was relayed directly from the target spotter on the ground to the aircraft, where it was automatically used by the aircraft's fire control and navigation computers. This equipment eliminated the need for voice communications, which can be jammed or misunderstood. Besides improving the aircrew's chances of survival during close air support operation, such precise communications allow the target to be destroyed in a single high-speed, low-altitude pass to retain the element of surprise. When two passes must be made to destroy a target, the enemy has a

*The AFTI/F-16 has been a successful and long-running test bed for a multitude of new fighter technologies.*

much better chance to shoot down the aircraft with surface-to-air weapons during the second pass.

These tests were conducted at Edwards AFB, Fort Irwin, and the Superior Valley Tactical Range, all located in California, and in cooperation with the U.S. Army. Data was relayed to an Army OH-58 helicopter to the FAC to the AFTI/F-16. During these flight tests, which ran in the spring and summer of 1988, the AFTI/F-16 was also used to check out new technologies such as an automated digital terrain management and display system for navigation, an integrated flight and fire controls for automated standoff weapon delivery, a conformally-mounted infrared laser sensor tracker, a helmet-mounted sight, and a new digital flight control system.

By 1991, a highly modified AFTI/F-16 should be flight-testing even more ambitious technologies that could be used in a next-generation close air support and battlefield interdiction (CAS/BAI) aircraft. The purpose of this next phase of the AFTI/F-16 program is to develop and flight-test technologies that enhance an aircraft's ability to find and destroy enemy ground targets day or night. The developments make maximum use of the F-16's maneuverability at high speeds and low altitudes, plus its electronic "stealthiness" to survive against threats from enemy surface-to-air weapons.

One of the new technologies to be tested is an All-Terrain Ground Collision Avoidance System (GCAS) that will keep an aircraft from flying into the ground regardless of its flight altitude. The GCAS uses digital terrain data and real-time data from a forward-looking sensor. The AFTI/F-16 also incorporates a Maneuvering Terrain Following/Terrain Avoidance/Threat Avoidance (TF/TA/ThA) system that allows both manual and automated 5G maneuvering.

For enhanced night attack capability, the AFTI/F-16 uses an ejection-safe integrated helmet system that incorporates image intensification or night vision capability, FLIR images of the pilot's view of the world, and overlays of HUD information. Unlike the

*The AFTI/F-16's latest role is testing technologies for the Close Air Support (CAS) mission.*

*The F-16/CCV aircraft preceded the AFTI/F-16. It demonstrated that it was possible to increase the operational capabilities of future high-performance aircraft by designing their control systems for unconventional flight modes.*

present HUDs, which require the pilot to look straight ahead to monitor aircraft performance, this system allows the pilot to view aircraft performance while always keeping track of what is happening in any direction outside the cockpit.

Modifications to the bomb delivery system will allow delivery of ordnance while flying on a circular flight path over any type of terrain. An advanced Targeting FLIR will increase the target detection range and the ability to track multiple targets. By integrating the FLIR with the bombing and flight control computers, the AFTI/F-16 will be able to automatically deliver weapons on more than one target on each pass over the threat area.

Few flight test programs have been able to accomplish as many diverse objects as the AFTI/F-16. Some of the advanced technologies already found their way into manned fighters. Much more is still to come.

## F-16/CCV

Preceding the AFTI/F-16 program was the so-called CCV (Controlled Configured Vehicle) program, which used the Number One YF-16 prototype as the test aircraft. The purpose of the program was to demonstrate how the operational capabilities of future high-performance fighters could be greatly enhanced by designing their control systems so that they could perform some rather unconventional maneuvers.

Modifications made to the F-16's flight control system enabled pilots to shift their flight paths laterally or vertically without pitch or roll inputs. The pilots were also able to point the nose up and down without power changes, and left or right while maintaining a constant track over the ground.

There were also changes to the fuel systems, and two canards, canted at 30-degree angles, were mounted on the front of the fuselage. This same configuration would later be used on the AFTI/F-16 that would follow.

## VISTA

It might look like an ordinary two-seat F-16D Fighting Falcon, but the VISTA inflight simulator can fly like the Aerospaceplane, Advanced Tactical Fighter, or, for that matter, just about any other aircraft that the engineers might want to simulate. VISTA stands for Variable Stability Inflight Simulator Test Aircraft.

The VISTA simulator's flight controls can be "reconfigured" electronically through programming of its variable stability system to try out new aircraft concepts inexpensively and safely without having to build a special prototype. The VISTA lets pilots learn how a new airplane will handle before flying the new airplane itself.

The VISTA flies like the aircraft being simulated, and not like an F-16. Furthermore, the VISTA can realistically simulate the diverse forces that would be acting on the simulated aircraft, along with how the aircraft would respond to these forces. The pilot thinks he is flying the simulated aircraft, obtaining the correct information, feedback, and "feel."

Besides trying out new flying characteristics, the VISTA will be used to test pilot reactions to new cockpit displays and advanced avionic systems. The VISTA can be set up to fly with either a center or sidestick controller, the latter being used in the normal F-16. All controls—stick, throttle, rudder pedals, and displays—will be operated through the variable stability computer so their characteristics can be altered—mainly by software changes.

In recent years there has been considerable interest in forward-swept wings for fighter aircraft. Forward-swept wings have several advantages including lower stall speeds, improved spin characteristics, and better low-speed flying qualities. This artist's concept of an F-16 with forward-swept wing will probably never happen.

Artist's drawing of the FS-X, an aircraft that once was planned for codevelopment and coproduction by the U.S. and Japan. It would have used the F-16 as the baseline.

*An F-16 being refueled in flight.*

*An F-16 launching a missile.*

*An F-16 in low-level flight.*

*Two F-16s reaching for the skies.*

*Much advanced fighter technology has been tested
in the highly successful AFTI/F-16 program.*

An inflight simulator is better than a ground-based simulator because it offers much more realism. By actually flying, the pilot can actually see and feel how the aircraft handles and responds to control inputs.

The VISTA began life as an F-16D. Its key modifications include the addition of the reconfigurable flight controls and the variable stability computer. Because of the severe maneuvers possible, even over and above those that might be experienced by an F-16, the VISTA uses heavy-duty hydraulics for moving the flight control surfaces.

Unlike the normal two-seat F-16D, in which the aircraft's command pilot rides up front, the VISTA's rear seat is the "command" cockpit with the front seat being the simulation cockpit. From here, the test pilot will fly the simulated aircraft, obtaining a better view of the world outside than that offered in the rear seat.

After flight testing, which should run through the summer of 1991, the VISTA will be used by the U.S. Air Force, the U.S. Navy, and NASA for aeronautical research and development. Current plans are to use the VISTA for the next 25 to 30 years. After all, VISTA will replace the NT-33A inflight simulator based on the Lockheed T-33 T-Bird trainer, which has been used for similar type testing for over 30 years.

USAF

*It might look like an ordinary two-seat F-16D, but the VISTA inflight simulator can fly like the Aerospaceplane, Advanced Tactical Fighter, or, for that matter, just about any aircraft the engineers might want it to be. VISTA stands for Variable Stability In-flight Simulator Test Aircraft.*

General Dynamics/Fort Worth is making the modifications to the F-16D while Calspan Corporation is responsible for the design and integration of the variable stability system. Bendix Corporation is supplying the digital flight control computers that are modified from those normally used in the F-16.

# 6

# Roles and Missions

T HE F-16 Fighting Falcon is an extremely versatile fighter. It is already being used as an air-to-air interceptor, air-to-ground attack fighter, and air-to-air superiority fighter. Other missions for the F-16 include reconnaissance and radar suppression. It serves as an advanced adversary aircraft for aircrew training and is the mount of the Thunderbirds precision flight team. The F-16 might also well be the replacement for the Fairchild A-10 in the Close Air Support/Battlefield Air Interdiction (CAS/BAI) role.

## Air Superiority and Ground Support

The Air Force has dubbed the F-16 the "Swing Force Fighter" due to its ability to perform equally well as an air superiority fighter and as an air-to-surface delivery system. For example, when returning from a ground support mission, the F-16 can "swing" back to the air-superiority role. The F-16 was in fact originally optimized to be a superior air-to-air combat machine, but its high thrust-to-weight ratio and low wing loading make it superior for air-to-surface support as well.

Even though the F-16 is in the lightweight class, it still packs a big punch when it comes to armament carried. Extended range and the versatility of the weapons available add to the aircraft's potency. During air-to-air combat, the F-16's gun and air-to-air missiles would be used. For ground support work, the gun, rockets, and conventional bombs along with "smart" weapons (such as laser-and TV-guided bombs) are installed on the F-16, though the gun and air-to-air missiles are still retained to ward off an airborne enemy attack.

The M-61A1 Vulcan 20mm multibarrel cannon, built by General Electric, is located

## Air Superiority Mission

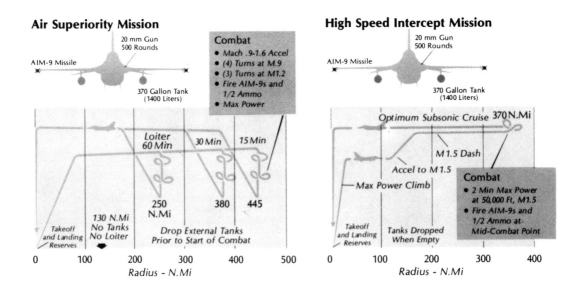

## High Speed Intercept Mission

## Close Air Support Mission

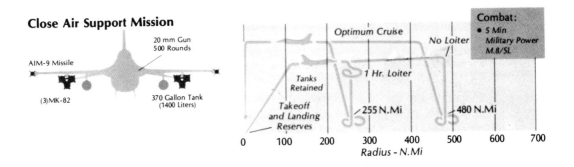

## Air-to-Surface Mission

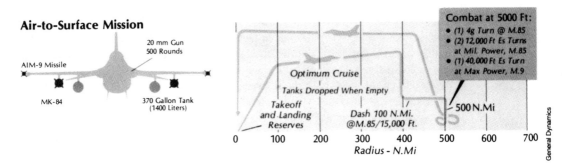

*Typical mission profiles for Air Superiority and Close Air Support role. These are actually for the F-16/79 that never reached production.*

*The F-16 was the first single-seat fighter to achieve accurate, unassisted delivery of a laser-guided weapon. Here a GBU-10 laser-guided bomb is delivered automatically at an altitude of 5,000 feet while traveling at 480 knots. The bomb followed a laser beam to the target. The laser designator pod is mounted on the right side of the engine inlet.*

in the fuselage just behind the pilot in the left wing/body fairing. This Gatling-type gun can fire at the rate of 6000 rounds per minute; 515 rounds are carried. The gun's "snapshot" gunsight is part of the head-up display (HUD).

On the wingtips, under the fuselage, and below the wings are pylons or hardpoints for carrying a wide assortment of weapons (or, in military jargon, *stores*). Normally, air-to-air missiles such as the Sidewinder are mounted on the wingtips. Up to four more Sidewinders can be carried on the outer underwing pylons.

For range extension, 300-gallon fuel tanks can be carried under the wings and dropped when their fuel load has been expended. With the drop tanks, the F-16 has a ferry range of over 2400 miles, allowing self-deployment overseas. With the normal fuel load, the radius of action is more than 575 miles.

The Fighting Falcon can carry the Martin Marietta Pave Penny laser spot tracker pod under the fuselage; pods that house ECM (electronic countermeasures) and chaff/flare dispensers can also be accommodated under the wings. In the future, the F-16 could carry advanced systems such as the Westinghouse/ITT AN/ALQ-165 airborne self protection jammer (ASPJ), advanced optical or FLIR sensors, and advanced beyond-visual-range missiles.

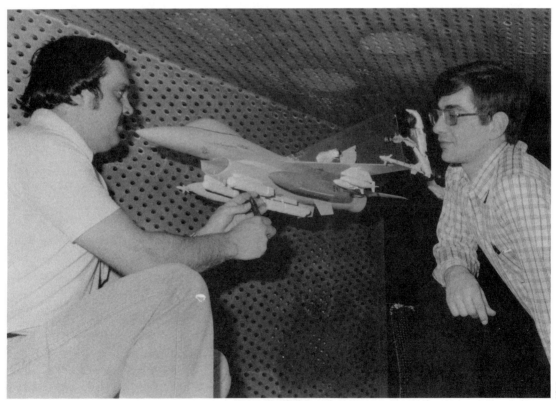

USAF

*Many tests were performed on different stores configurations of the F-16. Here, the aerodynamic effects of navigation and targeting pods are being investigated on a wind tunnel model.*

*Here an F-16 is being refueled by a KC-135.* USAF

The F-16 has already been used as the launching platform for a variety of weapons including the AMRAAM (Advanced Medium Range Air-to-Air Missile), Sidewinder, radar-guided Sparrow and Skyflash air-to-air missiles, the French Magic 2 infrared homing air-to-air missile, the Maverick air-to-surface missile, HARM and Shrike anti-radiation missiles for homing in on enemy radar installations, and the Norwegian Penguin Mk3 anti-ship missile. A 30mm gun has also been successfully fired from the fuselage gun station. The F-16 is ready to perform well into the 21st century.

The pilot can call upon several pieces of avionics to help in both the air-to-air and air-to-surface roles. First, there is the radar, which can be used in aerial combat, for weapons delivery in adverse weather, and for navigation. For air-to-air combat, the radar is capable of both air-to-air uplook for searching and tracking aircraft that are above the horizon, and for looking downward for aircraft with the ground in the background. Low-flying aircraft can be distinguished from ground clutter, the latter being eliminated to give a clean scope and easy recognition of targets. When the pilot closes in on his target, he can push the "dogfight" switch on the throttle and get into the automatic air combat search mode. In this air combat mode, the radar will scan through the HUD field of view, automatically acquire the first target that it encounters within the search area, and initiate automatic track of that target.

The radar also provides information through its computer for pointing the Sidewinder missile's target seeker. A lead-computing optical sight and snapshot displays on the HUD are used to accurately aim and fire the Vulcan 20mm cannon. During air-to-air combat, optimized energy maneuvering information is also provided on the HUD so that the pilot can obtain the maximum performance from his aircraft.

For air-to-surface use, the pilot can select several additional modes of operation simply by using a switch on the radar control panel. A real beam mapping mode gives the pilot an all-weather map of the ground in a selected area ahead of the aircraft. The map can be used for navigation, detection and location of ground targets, and for delivering weapons. The radar can be used in conjunction with a ground beacon for blind bombing.

*An F-16 on a conventional bombing run over a desert gunnery range.*

*One role considered for the F-16 was a "Wild Weasel" aircraft for disrupting ground-based enemy air defenses. Some of the modifications needed to do the job include wingtip antenna pods to detect enemy radars, Shrike and Standard ARM anti-radiation missiles, and an electronic countermeasures pod installation. The anti-radiation missiles home in on emissions from radar sites.*

**60**

*Two F-16s fitted with AIM-9J Sidewinders on their wingtips. The aircraft in the foreground is also carrying two MK 82 500-pound low-drag bombs on wing stations two and eight.*

An air-to-ground ranging mode allows real-time measurement of distance to a particular point on the ground. Information for this mode of operation comes from the aircraft's fire control computer, and this mode is used for surface weapon delivery. The F-16 also has the ability to launch and direct electro-optical guided weapons such as the Maverick.

There is even more electronics equipment aboard the F-16 to get the aircraft in and out of combat safely. There is a radar warning display that tells the pilot when an enemy radar is beamed at him—sort of a sophisticated "fuzzbuster." Various electronic countermeasures pods, chaff, and flares can also be used as penetration aids. Naturally, there is a full complement of navigation and communications equipment. The avionics—and, for that matter, all the systems—incorporate built-in, self-test, fault isolation and condition indicators. These items reduce time and manpower needed to find a problem and make repairs.

The design of the F-16 is in tune with the times. It is built with economy in mind, but it does not sacrifice performance or reliability. In fact, the F-16 is so reliable and has such a low out-of-commission rate that extra pilots are needed to keep it in the air. The aircraft's readiness could exceed the physical endurance of the pilots.

*Here a Maverick television-guided missile is fired from an F-16B.*

General Dynamics.

*Two infrared-guided Maverick air-to-ground missiles are mounted under each wing of a U.S. Air Force F-16.*

## Air Defense

Some 270 of the original F-16A/Bs are being modified into the F-16 ADF, or Air Defense Fighter. These are replacing the aging F-4s and F-106s used by Air National Guard Fighter Interceptor Groups in the continental United States. The first F-16 ADF was placed in service in 1989 and the last is expected to be delivered in 1992.

For this role, the APG-66 radar is being upgraded with an AMRAAM data link. The F-16 ADF will also be equipped with an improved ECCM and enhanced survivability against cruise missiles. Other new equipment includes upgraded radar to better detect small targets, an expanded avionics computer, an HF (high frequency) radio, an improved fire control system, an advanced IFF (Identification Friend or Foe) interrogator, an ID light, a crash-survivable flight data recorder, and provisions to interface with GPS (Global Positioning Satellite). The ADF version of the F-16 is armed with an M61 20mm gun and up to six air-to-air missiles including Sparrows, Sidewinders, and AMRAAMS, or combinations of all three.

## Thunderbirds

The USAF's Aerial Demonstration Squadron, better known throughout the world as the Thunderbirds, has been flying the F-16 since the 1982 show season. The F-16 replaced the Northrop T-38 Talon.

Although the Thunderbird's F-16s are painted in the traditional red, white, and blue team colors, they have no modifications that in any way affect the combat capability of the aircraft. If the need arises, the Thunderbird aircraft could be repainted and restored to com-

*Here an F-16 is test-launching a GBU-15 laser-guided bomb.*

bat configuration within 72 hours. Then the aircraft and pilots, along with the maintenance and support personnel, would be reintegrated into a combat-ready unit at Nellis AFB, Nevada. Because of this, aircrews not only have to practice aerobatic maneuvering, they must maintain their proficiency in air-to-surface tactics and air superiority maneuvering.

The F-16's range makes it possible for the Thunderbirds to fly their aircraft long distances—even overseas—for demonstrations, one of the reasons why they selected the F-16.

## Adversary Trainers

The USAF has been using the Fighting Falcon for its adversary training since early 1989. Thus F-16s wearing Soviet paint schemes like those of MiG-23 and MiG-29 fighters can be seen at Nellis AFB, RAF Bentwaters, England; Kadena Air Base, Japan; and Tyndall AFB, Florida. The F-16s are replacing the Northrop F-5 fighters as the aggressors in Red Flag training exercises.

The U.S. Navy uses 22 F-16Ns and four twin-seat TF-16Ns to simulate the latest Soviet fighters in air combat training. Since 1987, the Ns have been assigned at NAS Key West, the Naval Fighter Weapons School of "Top Gun" fame, and the VF-126 adversary

*The initial launch of the Advanced Medium-Range Air-to-Air Missile (AMRAAM) during flight tests at the White Sands Missile Range in New Mexico.*

squadron at NAS Miramar in California. The F-16N is a slightly modified version of the F-16C.

The F-16Ns are powered by a General Electric F110-GE-100. The airframe is beefed up a bit to handle the higher G forces encountered during adversary missions. Also, the M61 gun is deleted and only practice missiles are carried. However, the F-16N can carry the full complement of "real" weapons and external fuel tanks should the need arise.

*A Shrike being fired from an F-16.*

This, incidentally, was not the first time the F-16 was considered by the Navy. In the early days of the program, the F-16 was a serious contender in the VFAX program (later changed to the Navy Air Combat Fighter or NCAF) as a replacement for the McDonnell Douglas F-4 and LTV A-7. But the Navy finally settled on the F-18, which started out as a highly modified version of the YF-17. The F-16 proposed for combat duty with the Navy and Marine Corps was a considerably different aircraft to meet its seagoing role. Designated the Model 1601, it would have had a stretched fuselage and an uprated engine.

## Reconnaissance

F-16A(R)s have been used in a tactical reconnaissance role by the Royal Netherlands Air Force since 1983. Now the U.S. Air Force is looking at a recce version that could be deployed by the early 1990s. This version would require a minimum of changes to the existing F-16s, since pod mounted sensors would be used. The underbelly reconnaissance pod would include advanced electro-optical and infrared sensors for both day and night reconnaissance.

## Close Air Support

The F-16's next major mission could be as a close air support replacement for the A-10, providing firepower to support Army ground forces. The F-16 is competing against several other candidates, including the LTV A-7+ and perhaps even a completely new aircraft.

Any new CAS aircraft must be able to manage the multitude of tasks involved in support of troops on the ground and provide improved target acquisition. A new CAS fighter must be more lethal, allow easier use of weapons, and be able to operate at night or in adverse weather. Survivability is also an important issue with the requirement for high-speed, low-altitude, first-pass target kill being a top priority item for application in the battlefield environment of today and the foreseeable future.

Priority equipment for CAS/BAI mission includes an improved data link to aid accu-

*The Air Force Thunderbirds use F-16s that can be quickly reconverted to full combat-ready status.*

*The Thunderbirds' F-16s in close formation.*

*The Thunderbirds' distinctive color scheme can be quickly repainted in combat camouflage.*

rate target location, a digital terrain system for improved navigation, the Pave Penny laser targeting system, and a 30mm gun for better armor destruction capability. Selected hardening is needed for improved survivability. A head-steered forward-looking infrared (FLIR) sensor system with a helmet-mounted display would allow the pilot to operate at night using the same tactics as in the daytime.

Much of the technology for a CAS version of the F-16 has already been demonstrated in the AFTI/F-16 and an F-16B leased by General Dynamics that is used as a technology demonstrator. Additionally, the Tactical Air Command has demonstrated the F-16's current CAS capabilities using seven F-16Cs in tests at Nellis AFB, Nevada, and Fort Hood, Texas.

The Air National Guard has replaced its A-10s with F-16s at one CAS squadron in Syracuse, New York, where F-16A/B aircraft are being flown in operational proof-of-concept demonstrations. Modifications include a centerline-mounted 30mm cannon pod, a digital data link, and a Collins Automatic Target Handoff System. This equipment is being retrofitted into the 20 aircraft.

An upgraded F-16 CAS configuration is based on the Block 30 version of the F-16C/D. Modifications include Have Sync radio installation, a digital terrain system, an upgraded Pave Penny laser spot tracker, the 30mm gun pod, selected hardening, and an improved data modem consisting of a second-generation data link that interfaces with existing radios.

The latter equipment allows for target acquisition on the first high-speed pass with no voice communications needed between the FAC and attack aircraft. This not only greatly reduces pilot workload but also improves accuracy of information transfer, decreases vulnerability to jamming, and is much more secure. With a direct interface with the aircraft's

*What are Navy markings doing on this F-16? The Navy uses the F-16N, a modified F-16C, in adversary training for its "Top Guns."*

fire control system along with precise information from a navigation system, such as a digital terrain system supported by the Global Positioning System (GPS), very accurate targeting information can be displayed on the HUD. This information can also be used for controlling sensors or "smart" weapons such as the Maverick. General Dynamics is also

USAF

*A new digital data link was demonstrated by this AFTI/F-16 and Army OH-58D helicopter during the summer of 1988. The data link replaces voice communication between the close air support fighter and scout helicopters and forward air controllers.*

proposing that the onboard systems be used in conjunction with shoulder-held, man-portable automatic targeting systems on the ground for even more accurate targeting, especially against moving targets.

A digital terrain system would provide autonomous, precision navigation, dynamic terrain following, terrain and obstacle avoidance, and covert target ranging. Additional target acquisition and identification flexibility would be provided by the Pave Penny system. Ballistic hardening is also being considered to complement the F-16's inherent survivability, which results from its small size, high speed, maneuverability, system redundancies, Halon fuel inerting system, and rugged 9G structure. One low-cost addition might be dry bay fire extinguishers.

# USAF F-16s in Persian Gulf

---

A S THIS BOOK GOES TO PRESS, Operation Desert Storm, the military campaign to free Kuwait from Iraqi occupation, has just ended. The full story of the F-16's role in the operation will have to wait until the fourth edition of this book, but the following information is available at this time:

The total number of USAF F-16s deployed to the Persian Gulf is still classified, but the deployed units are known, as shown in the accompanying list. Eleven Fighting Falcons were lost during the hostilities; five F-16As were lost in combat, presumably to ground fire because the Iraqi Air Froce was conspicuously absent; four F-16As went down to noncombat causes, along with two F-16Cs.

The total number and nature of the F-16's missions is also classified at this time, though it can be safely assumed that the Falcons were used for air superiority, ground support, and precision bombing. More than 100,000 sorties of all kinds were flown by U.S. and Allied Coalition forces. It would be reasonable to estimate that at least several thousand sorties were flown by F-16s. No aerial victories have yet been credited to F-16s.

The following U.S. Air Force F-16 units participated in Desert Storm:
- 363 Tactical Fighter Wing, Shaw Air Force Base, SC
- 388 Tactical Fighter Wing, Hill Air Force Base, UT
- 401 Tactical Fighter Wing, Torrejon Air Base, Spain
- 347 Tactical Fighter Wing, Moody Air Force Base, GA
- 50 Tactical Fighter Wing, Hawn Air Base, Germany

In addition, the following Air National Guard F-16 units were deployed to the Gulf:
- 169 Tactical Fighter Group, McEntyre ANG Base, Columbia, SC
- 174 Tactical Fighter Wing, Hancock Field, Syracuse, NY

# Appendix

# F-16 Program Milestones
# Special Instance

| | | |
|---|---|---|
| Jan | 1991 | USAF F-16s used in combat for first time in Operation Desert Storm, the liberation of Kuwait. |
| Jun | 1990 | Egypt signs LOA for six F-16s in addition to 40 already ordered in its third F-16 purchase. |
| Jun | 1990 | Congress is notified that Portugal intends to purchase 20 F-16A/B aircraft. |
| May | 1990 | Bahrain F-16s arrive in-country. |
| Mar | 1990 | Bahrain receives first F-16C/D aircraft. |
| Jan | 1990 | Singapore F-16s arrive in-country. |
| Dec | 1989 | 2500th worldwide F-16 delivered. |
| Dec | 1989 | Indonesian F-16s arrive in-country. |
| Oct | 1989 | F-16 teams sweep Gunsmoke '89 bombing and munitions competition. |
| Oct | 1989 | F-16 team wins USAFE Excalibur VI bombing competition. |
| Oct | 1989 | Indonesia takes delivery of first F-16A. |
| Sep | 1989 | Pakistan signs for 60 additional F-16A/Bs. |
| Jun | 1989 | F-16 team wins TAC's Long Rifle V bombing competition |

| Jun | 1989 | First dedicated close air support (CAS) unit activated at Syracuse, New York. |
| May | 1989 | First launch of AIM-7 Sparrow missile from F-16C following successful F-16A testing. |
| May | 1989 | First F-16C Block 40 deployed to Luke AFB. |
| Mar | 1989 | F-16XL #1 returned to flight status and delivered to NASA. |
| Feb | 1989 | First F-16 Air Defense Fighter retrofit modification completed. |
| Feb | 1989 | First F-16 Aggressor delivered in MiG-29 Fulcrum paint scheme. |
| Jan | 1989 | First F-16s based in United Kingdom (RAF Bentwaters). |
| Jan | 1989 | Republic of Korea Air Force orders four additional F-16D aircraft. |
| Jan | 1989 | Greece receives first F-16s at Nea Anhialos Air Base. |
| Dec | 1988 | Block 50 development authorized after first Block 40 F-16 is delivered. |
| Dec | 1988 | Pakistan signs for 11 additional F-16A/Bs. |
| Dec | 1988 | Agile Falcon pre-development authorized. |
| Nov | 1988 | Hellenic Air Force takes delivery of first F-16C. |
| Sep | 1988 | F-16 fleet reaches two millionth flight hour with simultaneous flights by pilots from Belgium, Denmark, the Netherlands, Norway, and USAFE. |
| Jun | 1988 | Congress is notified that Malysia will buy six F-16A and two F-16B aircraft. |
| Jun | 1988 | Korea orders four F-16D fighter/bombers. |
| Jun | 1988 | Denmark, the Netherlands, and Norway sign a Memorandum of Understanding with the U.S. to take part in development and production of the Agile Falcon. |
| May | 1988 | Thailand takes delivery of first F-16A. |
| May | 1988 | Israel orders more than 60 F-16C and D aircraft. |
| Apr | 1988 | F-16 teams dominate TAC's Long Rifle IV competition at George AFB, California. |
| Mar | 1988 | DOD approves preproduction development plan for Agile Falcon, F-16 derivative. |
| Feb | 1988 | Singapore takes delivery of first F-16, which was also 2,000th F-16 delivered worldwide. |
| Dec | 1987 | Thailand signs LOA for six additional F-16 aircraft. |

| Oct | 1987 | Japan announces F-16 derivative selected for FS-X program. |
|-----|------|---|
| Oct | 1987 | NAS Key West activated with F-16Ns. |
| Oct | 1987 | Luke AFB AFRES unit activates with new Block 32 F-16C/Ds (first F-16C/D to Reserve forces). |
| Oct | 1987 | First Turkish F-16C/Ds arrive in-country in national celebration at Murted AB. |
| Oct | 1987 | F-16 teams dominate Gunsmoke '87, USAF's worldwide bombing competition. |
| Oct | 1987 | F-16 teams sweep USAFE Excalibur II. |
| Oct | 1987 | USAF Thunderbirds complete Pacific tour to 14 cities in 10 countries; first show in PRC, first Pacific tour in F-16, first Pacific tour since 1959. |
| Oct | 1987 | Kunsan AB, Korea, begins conversion to F-16C/Ds. |
| Oct | 1987 | Egypt signs LOA for 40 additional F-16C/Ds with AIM-7 capability. |
| Sep | 1987 | 432 TFW, Misawa AB, Japan, wins Sabre Spirit '87 (PACAF munitions competition). |
| Sep | 1987 | McConnell AFB activates with F-16A/Bs becoming the second ANG F-16 training site. |
| Sep | 1987 | AFTI/F-16 program team receives AFA's 1987 Theodore von Karman Award for most outstanding achievement in science and engineering. |
| Aug | 1987 | F-16 teams dominate TAC's Long Rifle III bombing competition. |
| Jul | 1987 | F-16 teams sweep USAFE's first Excalibur bomb competition. |
| Jul | 1987 | Spangdahlem AB, Germany, activates with F-16C/Ds joining the F-4G Wild Weasels on defense suppression hunter/killer teams. |
| Jul | 1987 | Proposal is made to USAF that a derivative of the F-16, the Agile Falcon, be codeveloped and coproduced in the U.S., Belgium, Denmark, the Netherlands, and Norway. |
| Jul | 1987 | Turkish Air Force receives first F-16 in rollout ceremony at Fort Worth. |
| Jul | 1987 | Thailand plans to acquire an additional six F-16 fighter aircraft. |
| Jun | 1987 | First Block 32 F-16C/Ds delivered to USAF for deployment to Luke AFB (AFRES) and Nellis AFB (57 TFW). |
| Jun | 1987 | First F-16Ns delivered to U.S. Navy for Naval Fighter Weapons School (Top Gun) and VF-126 adversary squadron at NAS Miramar. |

| Jun | 1987 | Great Falls, MT, activates, becoming second ANG F-16A/B air defense site. |
|---|---|---|
| Jun | 1987 | 19 TFS, Shaw AFB, sets new one-day squadron world record of 160 sorties in commemoration of squadron's 70th anniversary. |
| May | 1987 | 50 TFW, Hahn AB, Germany wins USAF Daedalian and Phoenix Awards for best maintenance unit in USAF and DoD, respectively. |
| Apr | 1987 | U.S. Navy introduces first F-16N at NAS Miramar. |
| Apr | 1987 | Misawa AB, Japan, begins conversion to F-16C/D and activates second squadron. |
| Apr | 1987 | First intercept of Soviet aircraft by F-16s in CONUS air defense role. |
| Apr | 1987 | Ramstein AB, Germany, converts to Block 30 F-16C/Ds. |
| Mar | 1987 | F-16 teams dominate TAC's Long Rifle II bombing competition. |
| Mar | 1987 | Bahrain signs LOA for 12 F-16C/D aircraft. |
| Feb | 1987 | First F-16C arrives in Israel to complement F-16A/B fleet. |
| Jan | 1987 | General Dynamics signs formal agreement with Hellenic Air Force for 40 F-16C/D aircraft for Greece. |
| Dec | 1986 | USAF F-16 fleet exceeds one million flight hours. |
| Oct | 1986 | USAF announces F-16A winner of Air Defense competition for 270 strategic interceptor aircraft for use with the Air National Guard. |
| Oct | 1986 | First F-16C arrives in Egypt after delivery ceremony in August. |
| Sep | 1986 | Second Multiyear Procurement agreement signed for 720 F-16C/D aircraft to be manufactured in Fiscal Years 1986-1989. |
| Sep | 1986 | First ANG unit activated for air defense role with F-16A replacing F-106 at Jacksonville, Florida. |
| Aug | 1986 | Indonesia signs LOA for 12 F-16A/B aircraft. |
| Aug | 1986 | USAF F-16 fleet exceeds 90 percent mission-capable rate for the first month, far exceeding TAC standard. |
| Aug | 1986 | F-16 crews sweep top positions in TAC's Long Rifle '86 bombing competition. |
| Jul | 1986 | 1,000th F-16—and the 1,572nd manufactured—is delivered to the USAF. |
| Mar | 1986 | Republic of Korea Air Force formally accepts delivery of first F-16D, becoming the 10th nation to fly the Fighting Falcon and the first outside the United States to receive the advanced F-16C/D. |
| Feb | 1986 | USAF increases its planned F-16 acquisition from 2,795 to 3,047. |

| Jan | 1986 | Worldwide F-16 fleet surpasses one million flight hours. |
|---|---|---|
| Dec | 1985 | Ramstein AB, West Germany (USAFE), becomes 28th base world-wide for F-16, first overseas for F-16C/D. |
| Oct | 1985 | F-16 units win six of top seven places in USAF Gunsmoke '85 competition. |
| Jul | 1985 | F-16 Fighting Falcon is based at Misawa, Japan, second site in PACAF. |
| Apr | 1985 | U.S. Congress is told that Thailand will receive 12 F-16A/B aircraft. |
| Feb | 1985 | Formal delivery of the 998th F-16 produced under the multinational coproduction program at Gosselies, Belgium. |
| Jan | 1985 | U.S. Navy selects F-16N as its adversary flight training aircraft. Initial buy is 14 with follow-on for 12 more. |
| Jan | 1985 | Singapore announces it will purchase F-16 aircraft. |
| Nov | 1984 | Greece announces decision to obtain 40 F-16s, ending long competition. |
| Sep | 1984 | AFTI/F-16 begins second phase of testing with new avionics and other systems. |
| Aug | 1984 | Denmark orders 12 additional F-16s after delivery of first 58 was completed. |
| Jul | 1984 | First F-16C delivered to USAF after initial flight June 19. |
| Jan | 1984 | Activation of first F-16 Air Force Reserve Base at Hill AFB, Utah. |
| Dec | 1983 | Long-lead funding is authorized for first of 75 additional F-16s for Israel. |
| Dec | 1983 | Dutch Parliament approves purchase of an additional 57 F-16s, bringing its total order to 213. |
| Nov | 1983 | Delivery of first F-16 aircraft to Venezuela. |
| Oct | 1983 | F-16 units place 1st, 2nd, and 4th in USAF-wide Gunsmoke '83 bombing and strafing competition. |
| Sep | 1983 | Turkey announces decision to buy 160 F-16 aircraft. |
| Sep | 1983 | Venezuela accepts first of 24 F-16 aircraft in ceremonies at Fort Worth. |
| Jul | 1983 | Activation of first F-16 Air National Guard Base, McEntire ANGB, SC. |
| Jul | 1983 | Delivery of 1,000th F-16 manufactured to Hill AFB, Utah. |
| Apr | 1983 | USAF aerial demonstration squadron, the Thunderbirds, fly first public show. |

| Apr | 1983 | Second USAFE F-16 base activated at Torrejon AB, Spain. |
| Feb | 1983 | Belgium agrees to purchase an additional 44 F-16s. |
| Feb | 1983 | Activation of Luke AFB, AZ, as a major F-16 pilot training base. |
| Nov | 1982 | Transition from T-38A to F-16 by USAF Thunderbirds is completed. |
| Oct | 1982 | Pakistan accepts first of 40 F-16 aircraft. |
| Oct | 1982 | F-16XL with two-place cockpit and GE F101 engine makes first flight. |
| Jul | 1982 | USAFE activates first F-16 base at Hahn AB, West Germany. |
| Jul | 1982 | F-16XL, a derivative of the Fighting Falcon, rolled out and makes first flight. |
| Jul | 1982 | AFTI/F-16 is flown for the first time. |
| Jun | 1982 | 200th F-16 assembled in Europe is delivered, 100 each from Fokker and SONACA/SABCA since the multinational production program was begun. |
| May | 1982 | Venezuela signs for purchase of 24 F-16s. |
| May | 1982 | U.S. Congress is notified that Egypt has signed an order for 40 additional F-16s. |
| Mar | 1982 | USAF announces that the F-16 will be flown by the Thunderbirds, the USAF flight demonstration squadron. |
| Mar | 1982 | Air National Guard and Air Force Reserve Units will begin receiving the F-16 in 1983, the USAF announces. |
| Mar | 1982 | Egypt accepts first six F-16s in-country. |
| Jan | 1982 | Egyptian Air Force accepts first of 40 F-16s in ceremonies at Fort Worth. |
| Dec | 1981 | Pakistan becomes ninth nation to purchase F-16s. |
| Dec | 1981 | Korea signs letter of agreement for 36 F-16s. |
| Sep | 1981 | USAF inaugurates first overseas F-16 base at Kunsan, Korea. |
| Aug | 1981 | F-16 destroys F-102 target drone during first guided launch of an all-weather AMRAAM radar-guided missile. |
| Jun | 1981 | F-16s win Royal Air Force precision bombing competition at Lossiemouth, Scotland, scoring 7,831 of a possible 8,000 points. |
| Mar | 1981 | Twelve Fighting Falcons return to Hill AFB, Utah, from Norway after completing USAF's first F-16 operational deployment overseas. |
| Feb | 1981 | F-16 launches first Advanced Medium Range Air-to-Air Missile (AMRAAM). |

| Feb | 1981 | First Fighting Falcon aerial refueling via KC-10. |
| Jan | 1981 | Belgian Air Force's 349 Squadron becomes first F-16 fighter squadron to qualify for North Atlantic Treaty Organization service in Europe. |
| Jan | 1981 | F-16/79 intermediate fighter completes development flight test program. |
| Dec | 1980 | First flight of F-16/101 development aircraft. |
| Oct | 1980 | F-16 officially attains initial operational capability—combat-ready status—with the U.S. Air Force. |
| Oct | 1980 | First flight of F-16/79 intermediate fighter. |
| Jul | 1980 | Israeli Air Force accepts first four F-16s in-country following an 11-hour, 6,000-mile ferry flight from Pease Air Force Base, New Hampshire. |
| Jul | 1980 | U.S. Air Force officially names the F-16 "Fighting Falcon." |
| Jun | 1980 | Egypt signs letter of agreement to receive 40 F-16s. |
| Mar | 1980 | Dutch Government announces plans to increase F-16 buy from 102 to 213 aircraft. |
| Jan | 1980 | Deliveries of first F-16s to the Danish, Norwegian, and Israeli air forces. |
| Jun | 1979 | Royal Netherlands Air Force accepts first F-16. |
| May | 1979 | Three F-16s complete four-month long environmental and operational test program in Europe. |
| May | 1979 | First Dutch-assembled F-16 completes maiden flight. |
| Jan | 1979 | Belgian Air Force accepts first F-16 produced by a European assembly line. |
| Jan | 1979 | Delivery of first operational F-16 to USAF's 388th Tactical Fighter Wing at Hill AFB, Utah. |
| Aug | 1978 | Israel announces plans to procure 75 F-16s. |
| Aug | 1978 | First production F-16 completes maiden flight. |
| Aug | 1978 | F-16 becomes first single-seat fighter to achieve accurate, unassisted delivery of laser-guided weapons. |
| Jul | 1978 | Assemblers attach first major European-produced F-16 components (wings from Belgium) to a USAF F-16. |
| Apr | 1978 | Second European assembly line opens at Fokker-VFW in The Netherlands. |

| | | |
|---|---|---|
| Feb | 1978 | First European F-16 assembly line opens at SONACA/SABCA in Belgium. |
| Nov | 1977 | F-16 prototype launches all-weather AIM-7F Sparrow missiles. |
| Oct | 1977 | Department of Defense endorses F-16 full-scale production. |
| Aug | 1977 | Maiden flight of first two-seat F-16 fighter-trainer. |
| May | 1977 | First F-16 nonstop, unrefueled flight across the U.S. |
| Jan | 1977 | USAF announces plans for an additional 738 F-16s. |
| Dec | 1976 | First flight of F-16 Number One. |
| Oct | 1976 | Rollout of F-16 Number One. |
| Jul | 1976 | First European coproduction contract signed. |
| Dec | 1975 | Assembly of F-16 Number One begins. |
| Aug | 1975 | F-16 manufacturing begins. |
| Jun | 1975 | Belgium, Denmark, Norway, and The Netherlands announce plans to buy 348 F-16s. |
| May | 1975 | First transatlantic flight. |
| Jan | 1975 | U.S. Air Force selects F-16 as its Air Combat Fighter; announces plans to procure at least 650 aircraft. |
| May | 1974 | First flight of YF-16 Number Two. |
| Feb | 1974 | First flight of YF-16 Number One. |
| Dec | 1973 | Rollout of YF-16 Number One. |
| Aug | 1972 | U.S. Air Force selects two prototype competitors, one of them submitted by General Dynamics, for Lightweight Fighter. |

# Index

# Other Bestsellers of Related Interest

**Aero Series, Vol. 37, BOEING 737**—David H. Minton

This book offers an accurate and complete historical record of the Boeing 737, including commercial uses, prototypes, variations, and military applications. More than 100 line drawings and photographs illustrate the 737 from every possible angle, showing wings, tails, engines, pylons, cockpit interiors, galleys, instruments, cabin layouts, and liveries in close-up detail. 80 pages, 8-page full-color insert. Book No. 20618, $10.95 paperback only

**Aero Series, Vol. 38, THE McDONNELL DOUGLAS OH-6A HELICOPTER**—Donald J. Porter

Developed in the early 1960s and still in service today, the OH-6A helicopter earned a reputation during the Vietnam War as a dependable, high-performance machine. Widely used as both an airborne ambulance and observation craft, the OH-6A was uniquely suited to its roles. Porter examines the OH-6A's birth, development, physical characteristics, current status, and combat roles. 94 pages, 8-page full-color insert. Book No. 20619, $10.95 paperback only

**Aero Series, Vol. 39, A-7 CORSAIR II**
—William G. Holder

Nicknamed "SLUF" (for Short Little Ugly Fellow), the A-7 Corsair II has received more than its share of verbal jabs—this in spite of performing its job better than possibly any other aircraft in military history. This tells the complete story of the A-7 Corsair II, from its inception in the mid-1960s to its present use, and details the aircraft's technical aspects, developmental phases, modifications, and combat history. 96 pages, 78 illustrations. Book No. 3452, $10.95 paperback only

**Aero Series, Vol. 41, THE GRUMMAN X-29**
—Steve Pace

This volume traces the history of the X-29 from the early forward-swept wing concept to the latest test flight results. The pages come to life as pilots recount their test flight experiences. Scores of photographs and to-scale line drawings explore the X-29's digital fly-by-wire control system, the power plant that's now a hallmark jet engine, and the aerolastic tailoring of advanced composite materials. 96 pages, 81 illustrations. Book No. 3498, $10.95 paperback only

**Prices Subject to Change Without Notice.**

## Look for These and Other TAB Books at Your Local Bookstore

## To Order Call Toll Free 1-800-822-8158
(in PA, AK, and Canada call 717-794-2191)

or write to TAB BOOKS, Blue Ridge Summit, PA 17294-0840.